A Beginners Guide to Mothing

By Christopher Kline

Butterfly Ridge Butterfly Conservation Center ltd.
17864 State Route 374
Rockbridge, Ohio 43149
www.butterfly-ridge.com

ISBN-13: 978-1-7346197-2-0

Table of Contents

Thank you to the late Ira Kline for his willingness to stay up until the wee hours of the morning looking at moths with me. Also thanks to Dr. Bruce Walsh of the University of Arizona for introducing me to the wonderful world of moths and The Mothing Mavericks in southeast Ohio for continually encouraging me in my mothing endeavors.

Are you a Moth-er?

Admittedly, mothing may not be for everybody. I never thought I was a moth-er until I invited Dr. Bruce Walsh to conduct the moth portion of a 24-hour BioBlitz at the Boyce Thompson Arboretum in Superior, Arizona in 2007. Observing the diversity and beauty of moths on that night was enough to convince me that I might be a moth-er.

If you enjoy observing beauty in nature; if you enjoy learning new things about the life around you and trailblazing new paths, then mothing is for you. Mothing is perfect for night owls as moth activity does not start in earnest at the sheet until normally 11 pm.

You may not be a moth-er if you don't like bugs, especially bugs flying all around you, landing on you, and getting in your hair. The cover of this book shows people wearing masks, as they photograph their favorite moths on the sheet. Yes, this was required because of coronavirus. On hot steamy nights in July it is encouraged, regardless of the coronavirus. I also began to wear ear plugs as well. If you have an opening, the bugs will find it!

But any annoyance or inconvenience created by the visitors to the sheet was far outweighed by their beauty and diversity. My hope is that this will be your experience as well.

How To Use This Book

This book is designed to introduce the reader to the most easily recognized moths in Midwest. Each moth that has been included, I have personally observed in the Midwest, with the exception of the Black Witch, which I have observed on many occasions in the desert Southwest. Within each description is a listing of common host plants for the moth species as well as tips to aid in the identification of each species.

In addition, for each species listed there is a timeline presented. The timeline represents the months March - November. The red bar represents the timeframe that the moth would be expected to be present in the Midwest based on data posted to BugGuide.net and the Moth Photographers Group at Mississippi State University, as well as personal experience.

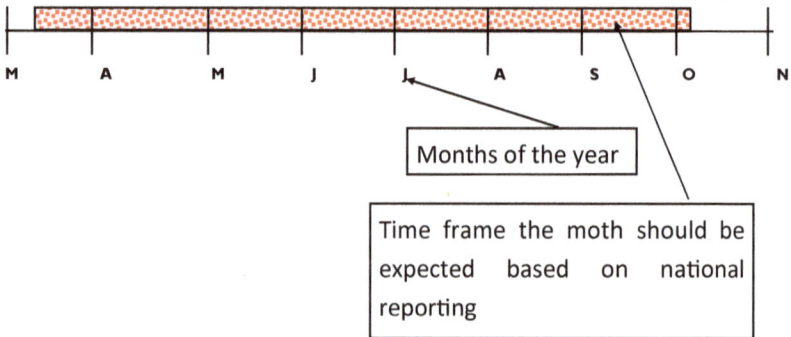

M   A   M   J   J   A   S   O   N

Months of the year

Time frame the moth should be expected based on national reporting

2

The descriptions for the moths will make more sense if you study the "About Moths" section of the book. This section will discuss the anatomy of the moth, including the names given to certain wing structures mentioned in the descriptions.

Colored arrows have been used in the book to emphasize certain identification features. The colors used for those arrows vary, and generally are chosen to make finding the arrows and structures easier.

Hodges Numbers
Each species of butterfly and moth is assigned a Hodges Number, based on the family and sub-family of each species. While the Hodges Number for a butterfly is rarely referenced, Hodges Numbers for moths are frequently used to help organize and discuss moths. The species represented in this book are arranged according to the Hodges Numbers for each species.

About Moths

Moths and butterflies are both in the insect order Lepidoptera. There are some keys differences between moths and butterflies. These are shown in the chart below and in the figures that follow. Keep in mind, there are exceptions for many of the rules that follow.

Characteristic	Moth	Butterfly
Active period	Nocturnal (night)	Diurnal (day)
Antennae	Feathery	Clubbed
Body	Heavy Hairy	Sleek Smooth
Pupal structure	Cocoon Or Pupa	Chrysalis
Resting position	Wings spread	Wings folded

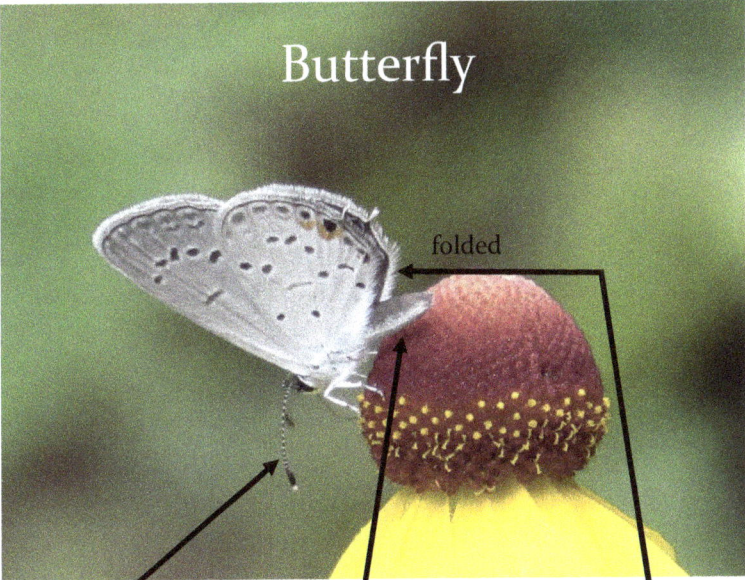

Butterfly

folded

Antennae   Body   Resting

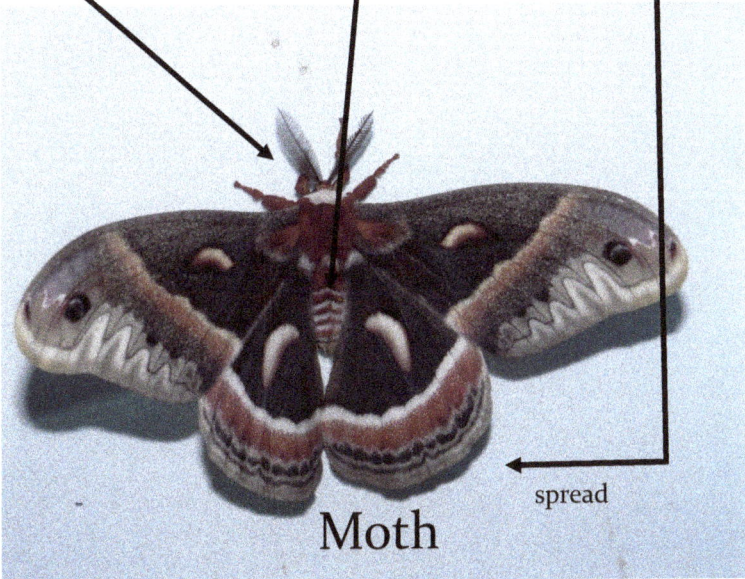

spread

Moth

Cocoon or Chrysalis

As shown previously, many moths pupate in a cocoon while butterflies pupate as a chrysalis. The photo below shows an Atlas Moth sitting on the cocoon it had emerged from. Butterfly caterpillars change into a chrysalis. On the bottom of the next page is a photo of a Monarch butterfly chrysalis.

The cocoon is created by the moth caterpillar, spinning silk from the outside in, such that the caterpillar is ultimately trapped within the cocoon. At that point, the caterpillar changes into a pupa inside of the cocoon. If one cuts into a cocoon they will find the pupa from which the moth will eventually emerge. Shown at the top of the next page is the pupa of a Hubbard's Small Silkmoth.

Atlas Moth and cocoon

Moth pupa

Some moths, the Sphinx Moths for example, do not spin a cocoon, but rather the caterpillar digs a hole in the soil and pupates underground.

Butterfly chrysalis

Moth Anatomy

This photo shows the different structures that are commonly used in moth identification.

Head

Thorax

Abdomen

Forewing

Hindwing

Legs (6)

Antennae

Ante-medial line

Reniform Spot

Post-medial Line

Another fun way to engage with moths is to search for their caterpillars. Many moth caterpillars fluoresce, or glow, when exposed to ultraviolet light. Ultraviolet flashlights are available through many online retailers.

We have found one of the best times to go caterpillar hunting is in late summer and early autumn. The photos below were taken in early October. Examining the trees and brambles may yield some exciting surprises. But be sure to watch out for the stinging hairs and spines that several moth caterpillars use for defense.

Pictured below is the same caterpillar under ultraviolet light and the standard camera flash.

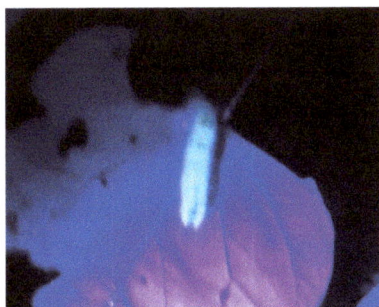

Attracting Moths

Since moths are largely nocturnal, special equipment is required to attract them for observation and study. While some people use the porch light as a tool to attract moths, I started with something more portable.

At Butterfly Ridge we started lighting with a portable scaffolding made from one-inch pvc pipe. We hung the sheet from the crossbar of the scaffolding and attached it to the scaffolding with black, foam pipe insulation.

As the pvc scaffolding aged, it started to loosen in the wind. Because of this, we built a wooden scaffolding that would be more stable in the wind. Below is a photo that shows the wooden scaffolding. It essentially looks like a wooden football goalpost.

Wooden mothing "goalpost" showing mercury-vapor light.

Attached in the middle of the "crossbar" on each side is a light. One side has an ultraviolet light, and the other side a mercury vapor light. The figure at the bottom of the page shows one of our ultraviolet bulbs.

We power the lights in two different ways. We can plug them into an extension cord run from a house or an outbuilding. We can plug in both lights simultaneously using a three-way adapter.

We also have a 2000 watt Honda generator that we can plug the lights into. The generator weighs only 30 pounds making it relatively portable and it can operate for about seven hours on a single tank of gas. By placing these mothing "goalposts" throughout the property, we are able to survey moths in a variety of habitats and locations.

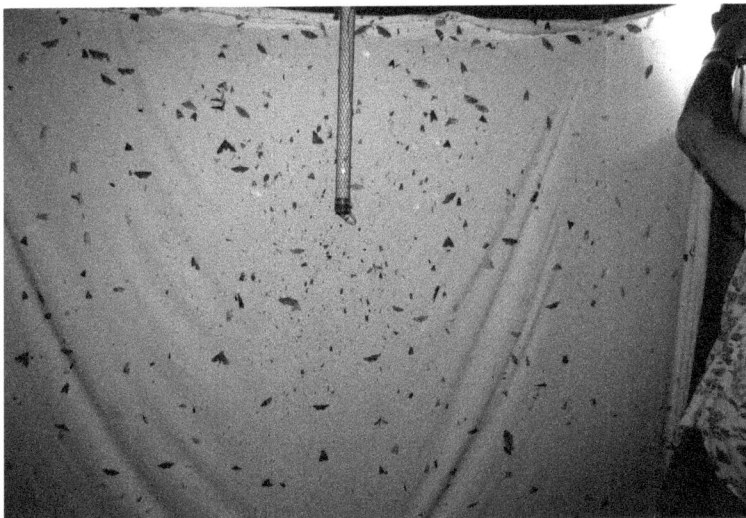

Ultraviolet light hanging from cross beam.

Moths, and also butterflies to a degree, can be attracted by painting a bait on tree trunks and stumps. The most common form of bait is a mixture of one-third dark, imported beer, one-third brown sugar, and one-third rotten fruit. Dark beers have more nutrients in them and imported beers do not have to be pasteurized, which would normally kill the fermentation causing organisms. For the fruit, we normally use rotting bananas. We also add yeast at a rate of one packet per half-gallon of bait. The bait works best when it is able to sit undisturbed for a few weeks prior to use. In the photo below you see a Julia Idia moth feeding on bait dripping down the side of a tree.

Julia Idia

Plants That Attract Moths

Since most moth larva feed on plant material, it is possible to influence moth diversity by altering plant diversity in the home landscape. Much like how folks create bee gardens and butterfly gardens, moth gardens can be designed and implemented into your landscaping plans.

Unlike butterflies, some of the best plants to attract moths are going to be trees. In the urban landscape with small residential lots, this may be tricky to work within. A large oak would easily overpower a small lot. In that case, perhaps smaller trees like dogwood and redbud would be better choices.

Appendix A in the back of this book provides the given host plants for the moths shown in this book as well as some of the more common moth species in the Midwest. Note that many moths are generalists, meaning they are not especially picky about their larval food plants. This will work considerably to your benefit.

Moths as Pollinators

Frequently moths are not thought of as pollinators. Granted, while they may not be the pollinating machines that bees are, moths do provide pollinating services.

Perhaps the most famous moth pollinator is *Xanthopan morgana*, also known as Morgan's Sphinx Moth. Morgan's Sphinx is the pollinator of the Darwin Orchid. This beautiful orchid has an extremely long spur and Darwin predicted that the pollinator of the orchid was a moth with nearly a foot-long proboscis.

The Darwin Orchid with the long spur extending from the lower left. (Photo: David Brigner)

Darwin was much ridiculed for putting forth the idea that a moth could have such a long proboscis. However, over 40 years after Darwin's prediction, Morgan's Sphinx Moth was observed pollinating the Darwin Orchid.

While southeast Ohio does not have such tall tales of pollinating moths with enormous proboscises, our moths perform the service of pollination all the same. The most common example of this is normally found during the daytime hours as the clearwing moths visit long tubular flowers as shown by the photo of the Hummingbird Clearwing Moth.

Hummingbird Clearwing Moth

Common Looper Moth

For an example of nocturnal moths performing pollination, visit a blooming patch of Common Milkweed some evening. Above is a photo of a Common Looper Moth visiting Common Milkweed around 10pm on a June evening. This particular milkweed patch was being visited by several species of Owlet Moths as well as a Grass-veneer Moth.

What are Micromoths?

Micromoth is the term that is applied to moth species with Hodges Numbers between 0000 and 6234. Most of the moths in this group are quite small, sometimes no longer than a quarter-inch. However, some members of the micromoths, for example the Carpenterworm Moths, can be well over an inch long.

The micromoths are frequently overlooked due to their small size. They can easily be presumed as a speck of dirt or debris on the sheet. However, with closer inspection, the careful observer will be rewarded with beautiful colors in bold, contrasting designs. The micromoths are every bit as beautiful as any other group of moths or even butterflies.

Moth Myths

Moths have a significant public relations problem. There are many myths out there that put moths in a negative light. Let's refute many of those myths:

1. **All Moths Eat Clothes**. Of the thousands of moth species native to North America, there are only three who tend to damage clothing; the Common Clothes Moth, Case-bearing Clothes Moth, and Carpet Moth.
2. **Moths Bite**. In fact, many species of moths do not have functioning mouth parts. They do not feed on anything. Those who do have mouths have a proboscis which is designed to sip nectar from flowers. Moths are physically not able to bite.
3. **Moths are Harbingers of Death**. This myth is drawn from Central American folklore which claims that the presence of a Black Witch moth in the house means someone will die. The Black Witch is no different than any other moth and cannot predict death.

Black Witch

4. **Moths Spit**. Once again, moth mouths are designed to suck nectar, not spit.

5. **Female Moths Shoot Eggs at People**. While it is true that female moths are not always picky about what they lay eggs upon, they do not launch eggs as a defense mechanism. But they will lay eggs on almost anything!

6. **All Moths are Pests**. While there are some moth species that are agricultural and forest pests like Gypsy Moth and Corn Earworm Moth, an over-whelming majority of moth species live as a part of nature, providing pollinating services and food for other organisms of nature.

7. **Moths are Little, Brown, and Ugly**. Check out any page of this book to refute this myth!

Moth Trivia

1. How many species of moths are there?

    a. On my twenty-one acre property in south-east Ohio we have documented 750 species. Ohio is estimated to have 3000 species. North America is estimated to have 10-15,000 species. The world is estimated to have 160,000 species.

2. What is the largest moth in the world?

    a. The Atlas Moth, found in Asian forests, has a wingspan approaching 12 inches.

3. What is the smallest moth in the world?

    a. *Stigmella maya* of Mexico has a wingspan of roughly one-tenth inch.

4. How many eggs can a female moth lay?

    a. The Gypsy Moth female is believed to lay close to 1000 eggs in her lifetime. A more reasonable average for moths in general is about 400.

5. What do adult moths eat?

    a. Most moths drink nectar from flowers. A few moths, especially the silkmoths, do not feed at all as adults. Then there are the Vampire Moths (genus *Calyptra*) that do in fact drink vertebrate blood.

6. What is the most beautiful moth?

    a. While beauty is in the eye of the beholder, I know the Madagascar Sunset Moth would get several votes!

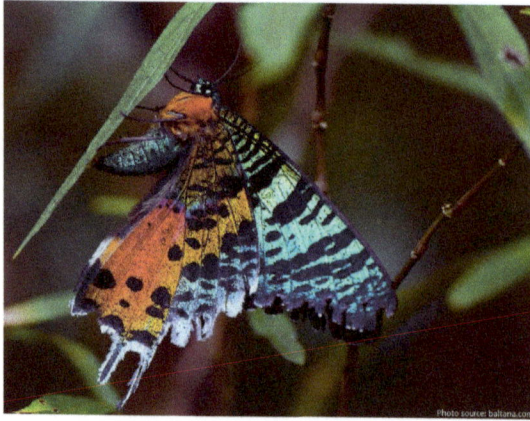

Photo source: baltana.com

7. What is the most famous moth?

    a. The Luna Moth can certainly lay claim to this title as the mascot for the drug Lunesta. The Death's Head Hawk Moth also received great fame from the movie Silence of the Lambs.

Learning to Identify Moths

Learning to identify moths will be one of your greatest challenges in becoming a moth-er. The trick will not be to memorize every moth in your area, but rather to begin recognizing groups of moths.

This process began for me when I attended a mothing weekend in extreme southern Arizona. There were several moth experts at this event. On the second morning of the event one of the participants was nice enough to borrow from different collections to create a map to the different groups of moths to help me start learning.

My Arizona moth map!

While a specific group of moths may contain numerous species, all of those species will have a certain "look" in common. As example, there are dozens of different species in the Underwing group (Genus *Catocala*), but all Catocalas have gray/brown forewings and colorful hindwings. So while you may not know which Underwing you are looking at, it will be easy to recognize that the moth belongs to that group.

Some of the micromoth groups are difficult to see a group-wide pattern in shape or design. In large part, that is because they are so small that any unifying features are hard to recognize. However, there are some exceptions such as the Leafblotch Miner group. While they are quite small, a behavior that many have in common is taking a "push-up" position at rest.

In the next few pages I will introduce you to some of these more easy to recognize groups of moths. Familiarity with the groups will make identification to species much easier.

Genus *Caloptilia* - Leafblotch Miner Moths

These micromoths are easily identified by the push-up position in conjunction with the furry femur on the legs.

Genus *Cosmopterix*

This genus of micromoth is consistent is having a broad orange band on the dark background, as well as metallic silver stripes on the wings.

Slug Moths

The slug moths are uniquely shaped. Picture the "pup tent" of your youth. Slug moths are "pup tent" shaped and frequently the abdomen extends beyond the wings.

Grass-veneer Moths

The grass-veneer moths, of which there are several species, are all shaped the same and are generally of light color but with different wings designs.

Genus *Pococera* - Webworm Moths

This genus Pococera has a narrow heart-shape with a mask across the middle of the forewings. These features are consistent across the group.

Plume Moths

The plume moths are uniquely designed. The wings are very narrow and held perpendicular to the body.

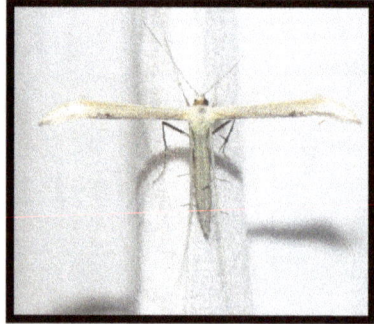

Geometrid Moths - Hodges #6256 - 7648

Many of the geometrids, but certainly not all, have scalloped wing edges, looking like they were cut with pinking sheers.

Sphinx Moths

The sphinx moths are normally easy to recognize. First of all, they are large, approaching two inches from "head-to-tail".

Sphinx's come in two forms. The first has more rounded forewing tips such as the above left photo. The other form has forewings that are squared off, like the bottom photo. In both forms the abdomen can be quite large and frequently is striped.

Tiger Moths

Most of the tiger moths have forewings that over-lap when the moth is at rest, completely conceal-ing the abdomen from view. While several of the micromoths do this as well, the tigers are the only large moths that reliably do this.

Zale Moths

The zales are a sub-group of the Noctuid moths. The zales normally hold their wings spread and flat, fully exposing the hindwings and the abdomen. The wing edges are also usually scalloped.

Underwing Moths

Another Noctuid sub-group, the underwings have gray-brown forewings with a variety of squiggly lines. The hindwings are frequently boldly marked and colorful, however the way they hold their wings rarely exposes the beautiful hindwings.

Good moth identification books are few and far between. Peterson has a good moth field guide, but it covers the entire northeastern portion of the country, which includes a huge number of moths. For a beginner, I would suggest a more local guide if possible.

To aid in identifying moths, there are a few online resources which can be very helpful. The Mississippi State Moth Photographers webpage (mothphotographersgroup.msstate.edu) can be a good source to confirm your identifications or to use after you have nailed down the identification to a particular group.

There is an app that can be used with your phone called Leps by Fieldguide which is very good, but not perfect. Hence the reason why learning the major groups of moths is so important, so that you will know when the app is pulling your leg, so to speak.

Perhaps the best way to learn your moths is to find a group of friends or local nature center which routinely does mothing. These folks can help guide your learning.

100

of the

Most
Recognizable Moths
in the Midwest

1046 – Epicallima argenticinctella
Orange-headed Epicallima Moth

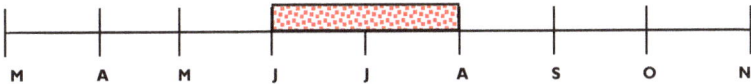

M	A	M	J	J	A	S	O	N

Host: Unknown, but elm is suspected. There are reports that it has been raised on corn.

Range: Throughout the Ohio Valley and Great Lakes.

Habitat: Found in a variety of habitats.

Identification: Very little is known about this moth. With a wingspan of about a centimeter, this is one of the most colorful of the micromoths.

2295 – *Dichomeris flavocostella*
Cream-edged Dichomeris Moth

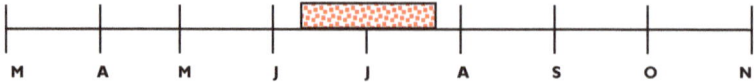

| M | | A | | M | | J | | J | | A | | S | | O | | N |

Host: Aster, sunflower and goldenrod.

Range: Found throughout the Midwest, south of Minnesota.

Habitat: Found primarily in open fields where the host plants are present.

Identification: The cream-colored edges on the black background of this micromoth are very unique.

2366 – *Plutella xylostella*
Diamondback Moth

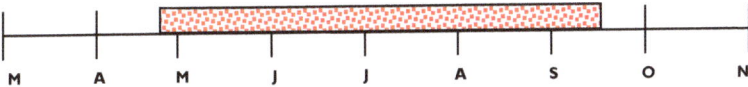

M   A   M   J   J   A   S   O   N

Host: The Mustard family of plants including cress, cabbage, radish, and broccoli.

Range: Found throughout the Midwest.

Habitat: Found in a wide variety of habitats.

Identification: This micromoth resembles its larger cousin the grass moths. The outline of the diamonds on the back is very unique. This moth is believed to have been introduced from Europe in the mid 1800's. The timeline above likely represents at least three generations per year.

2401 – *Atteva aurea*
Ailanthus Webworm Moth

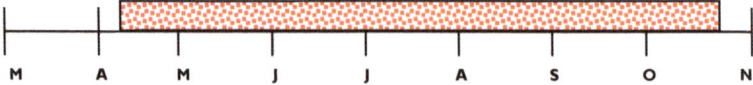

M   A   M   J   J   A   S   O   N

Host: Tree of heaven and sumac.

Range: Common in the East and the southern Plains.

Habitat: A wide variety of habitats including fields and woodland edges.

Identification: The orange stripes on the back and white checkerboard background is unlike any moth in our area. Possibly one of the most common moths in the Midwest, at times coming to the sheet by the hundreds. While this moth is native to the U.S., its primary host plant, tree of heaven, is an introduction from Asia.

2554 - *Synanthedon acerni*
Maple Callus Borer Moth

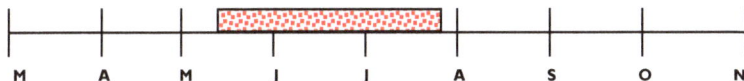

M	A	M	J	J	A	S	O	N

Host: Maple.

Range: Throughout the east but most common in Ohio, Indiana, and Illinois.

Habitat: This moth is commonly found in relatively open areas within maple forests.

Identification: This is a wasp mimic. Look for the black wing stripes and tuft of orange hairs at the tip of the abdomen. This moth is regularly seen, albeit in low numbers, in late spring and early summer. The caterpillars bore into maple trees to feed, as the tree forms a callus around them.

2693 - *Prionoxystus robiniae*
Carpenterworm Moth

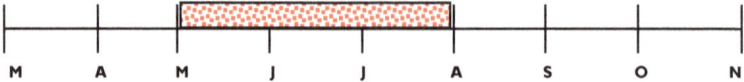

Host: Black locust, oak, maple, and other tree species.
Range: Ohio River Valley and Lower Great Lakes.
Habitat: Woodland edges.
Identification: Technically this is considered a micromoth, despite having a wingspan of nearly two inches. Initially this large moth may look like a member of the sphinx moths. The strongly reticulate (veiny) pattern of the wings is unlike any of the sphinxes. The larva of this moth is considered a forest pest, as it bores into the living wood of large trees.

3438 - *Grapholita eclipsana*
Solidago Root Borer

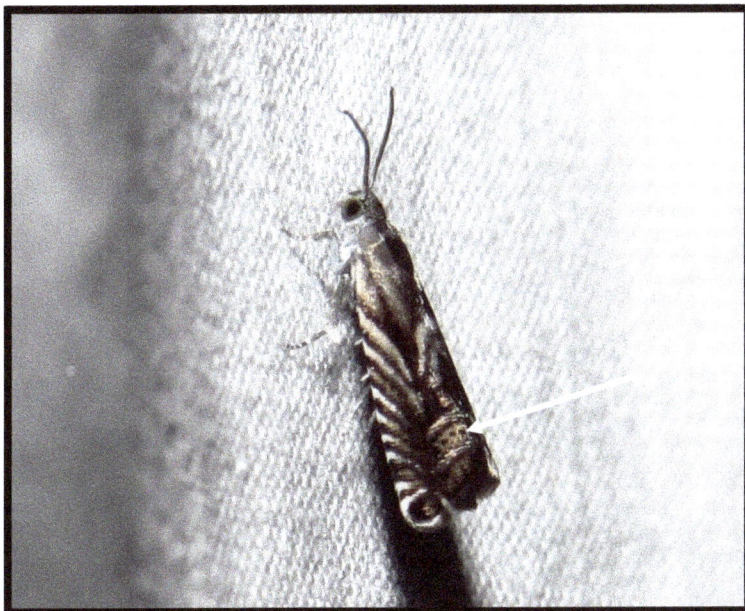

```
M       A       M       J       J       A       S       O       N
```

Host: Despite this moth's common name, the host plant is listed as false indigo. (*Amorpha*). *Solidago* is the scientific name for goldenrod, and since the site where I have seen this moth has no *Amorpha*, I will stick with goldenrod.

Range: Primarily the Ohio River Valley.

Habitat: Woodland edges and openings.

Identification: This is micromoth is very unique with its zebra striping throughout the forewing. It also has a bronze belt near the margin of the forewing (white arrow).

3494 - *Clydia latiferreana*
Filbertworm Moth

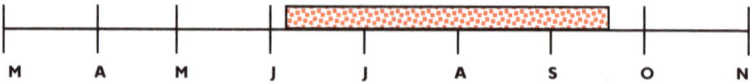

Host: Fruit of oak, beech, and possibly filbert.

Range: In the Midwest, it is most common in the Ohio River Valley.

Habitat: A variety of habitats including fields and woodland openings and edges.

Identification: This micrmoth is easily recognized by the silver-metallic stripes (black arrow) on the rust-colored base of the forewings.

3624 - *Argyrotaenia alisellana*
White-spotted Leafroller Moth

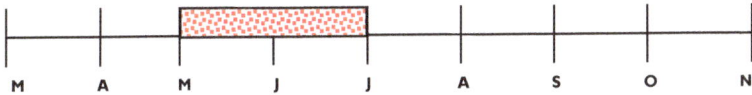

Host: Oak

Range: Throughout the Midwest

Habitat: Woodland edges and openings.

Identification: This micromoth has a very bold and unique pattern. Imagine white paintball splats on a chocolate brown background and you have White-spotted Leafroller. Little is known about this tiny moth.

3720 - *Cenopis reticulatana*
Reticulated Fruitworm Moth

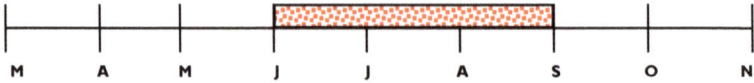

Host: Several species of deciduous trees.

Range: Throughout the Midwest.

Habitat: Woodland edges.

Identification: The reticulate, or net-like, appearance of the wings is very unique. The color, orange-yellow, is also unique and hard to miss, even for a micromoth. Some of the veins are thicker and darker in color.

3747 - *Coelostathma discopunctana*
Batman Moth

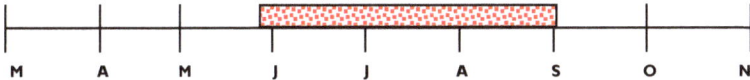

M   A   M   J   J   A   S   O   N

Host: Unknown.

Range: The Ohio River Valley to the lower Great Lakes.

Habitat: A variety of habitats including field, wetlands, and woodland openings.

Identification: Looking at this micromoth upside-down might make visualizing the "Batman" common name a little easier. For having such a colorful name, there is very little that is known about this moth.

4639 - *Pyromorpha dimidiata*
Orange-patched Smoky Moth

```
M      A      M      J      J      A      S      O      N
```

Host: Leaf litter.
Range: Ohio River Valley
Habitat: Woodland clearings and edges.
Identification: This moth is thought to be a Lycid beetle mimic. The feathery antennae of the Smoky Moth distinguishes it from the beetle. Similar also to the Black and Yellow Lichen Moth which is found in our area, but has much more yellow wings.

4644 - *Lagoa crispata*
Black Waved Flannel Moth

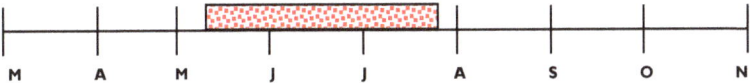

M	A	M	J	J	A	S	O	N

Host: Several deciduous tree species.

Range: Ohio River Valley

Habitat: Woodland edges and especially open fields.

Identification: The black splotching on the side separates this species from other flannel moths. Flies early in the evening. It is believed that the adult moths do not feed. Caterpillar (right).

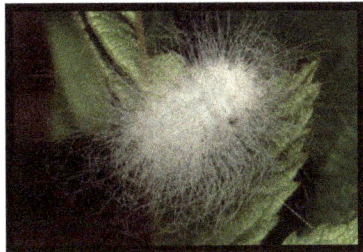

4669 - *Apoda biguttata*
Shagreened Slug Moth

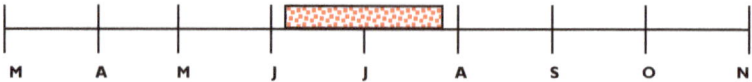

M A M J J A S O N

Host: Ironwood, hickory, and oak.
Range: Ohio River Valley and lower Great Lakes.
Habitat: A variety of habitats including fields, wetlands, and woodland edges.
Identification: The thick silver 'y' on each forewing is unique among our slug moths.

4671 - *Prolimacodes badia*
Skiff Moth

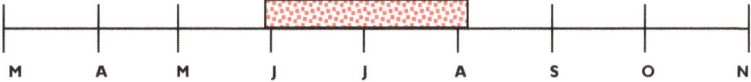

| M | A | M | J | J | A | S | O | N |

Host: A wide variety of deciduous trees and shrubs.

Range: Ohio River Valley to the lower Great Lakes.

Habitat: Despite the caterpillars feeding on a variety of tree leaves, we normally see this moth in open fields.

Identification: The dark brown half-moon on the light brown background is distinctive. However, while not the same design, this moth shares the same basic color pattern as the Arcigera Flower Moth (Hodge #11128) which flies later in the season. The common name of this moth is apparently a reaction to the shape if its caterpillar, resembling a skiff (flat-bottomed boat).

4675 - *Isochaetes beutenmuelleri*
Spun Glass Slug Moth

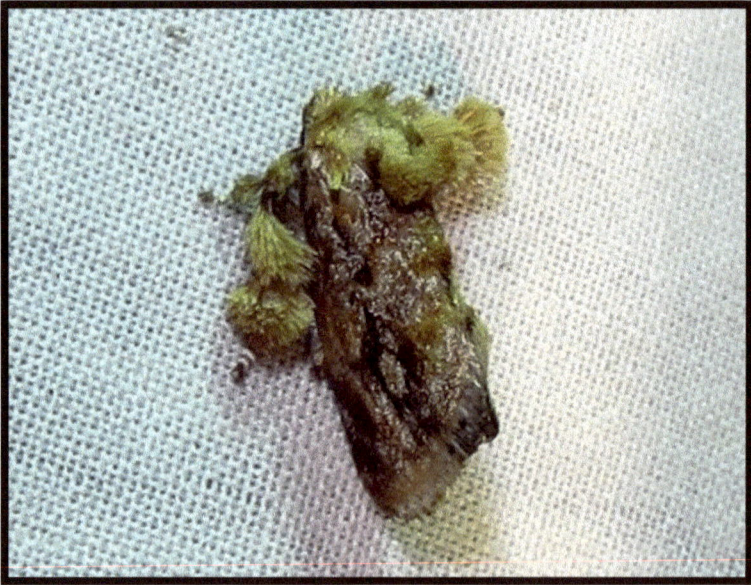

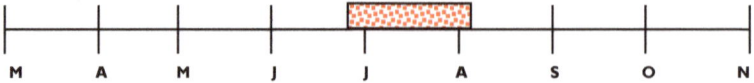

M   A   M   J   J   A   S   O   N

Host: Swamp Oak.
Range: Ohio River Valley.
Habitat: Open fields and woodland edges.
Identification: Most references list Swamp Oak as the host plant, however I have consistently observed this moth many miles from the nearest Swamp Oak, so there must be another host. I would expect that it hosts on several oak species. The 'brushy' appearance of the legs is distinctive. The common name is derived from the appearance of the caterpillar.

44

4697 - *Euclea delphinii*
Spiny Oak-slug Moth

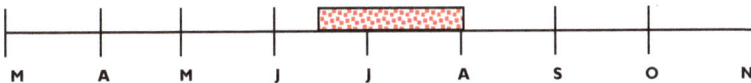

M	A	M	J	J	A	S	O	N

Host: A wide variety of deciduous trees and shrubs.

Range: The Ohio River Valley to the central Great Lakes.

Habitat: A variety of habitats including open fields, woodland edges, and wetlands.

Identification: This moth has one larger green triangle toward the base of the forewing, and another, much smaller, green triangle toward the apex of the wing.

4698 - *Parasa chloris*
Smaller Parasa Moth

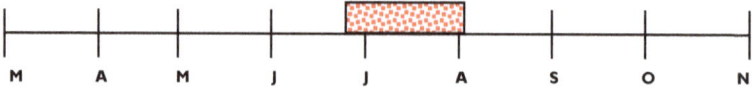

M	A	M	J	J	A	S	O	N

Host: Apple, dogwood, elm, and oak.
Range: Ohio River Valley
Habitat: A variety of habitats including open fields, wetlands, and woodland edges.
Identification: This slug moth has a broad green post-medial band, to go along with its green head and "back". No other moth in the Midwest has green in this arrangement.

4700 - *Acharia stimulea*
Saddleback Caterpillar Moth

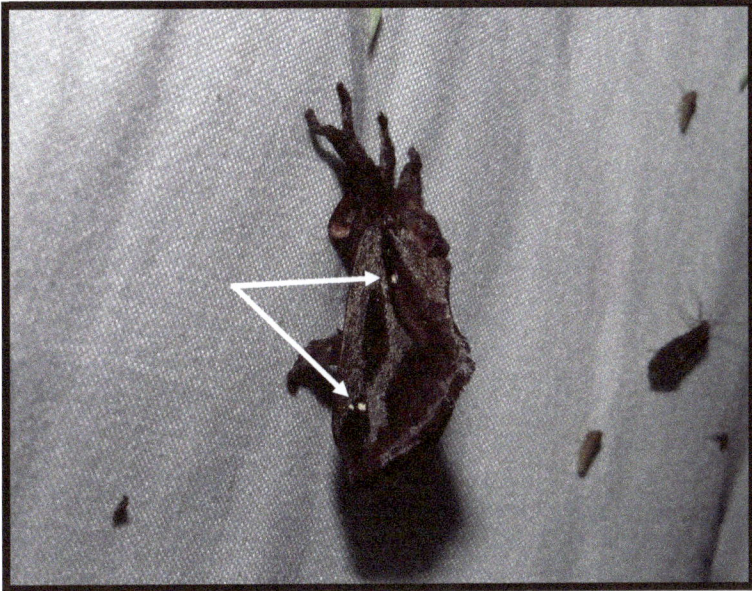

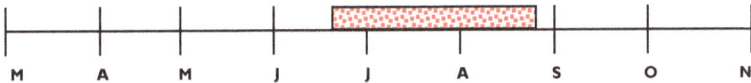

Host: Several deciduous tree and shrub species.

Range: Ohio River Valley and lower Great Lakes.

Habitat: A variety of habitats including open fields and woodland openings and edges.

Identification: Chocolate brown. Some have silver spots in the locations of the white arrows. This species also has one of the most unique looking of all caterpillars. Careful, the caterpillar's stinging cells pack quite a punch.

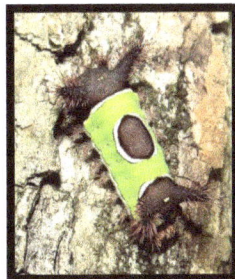

4744 - *Chrysendeton medicinalis*
Bold Medicine Moth

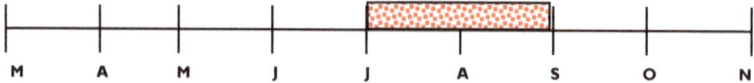

M · A · M · J · J · A · S · O · N

Host: Assumed to be grasses since it is in the Grass Moth Family, but otherwise no information is available.
Range: Ohio River Valley
Habitat: Open fields and woodland edges.
Identification: This micromoth was first described in 1881 and apparently has not been looked at since. Very little information is available for this boldly marked moth.

5040 - *Pyrausta bicoloralis*
Bicolored Pyrausta Moth

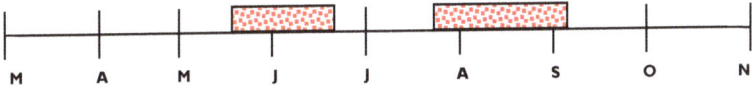

Host: Thought to be members of the Mint Family of plants.

Range: Ohio River Valley and Great Lakes.

Habitat: A variety of habitats including wetland, open fields, and woodland edges where host plants would be available.

Identification: This species is easily recognized by the two-toned wings; brick red toward the apex, orange toward the body. Also note the white fringe on the wings. This moth has two distinct generations, one in late spring, the other late summer.

5073 - *Pyrausta niveicilialis*
White-fringed Pyrausta Moth

```
|----+----+----▨▨▨▨----+----+----▨▨▨▨----+----|
M    A    M    J    J    A    S    O    N
```

Host: Unknown, however many of the *Pyrausta*'s use mint as a host.

Range: Ohio River Valley and Lower Great Lakes

Habitat: Unknown

Identification: This is one of the more uniquely designed grass moths with dark forewings and a white fringe. The shape of the moth is classic grass moth, to separate it from other dark moths. The white fringe on the forewing ends toward the apex of the wing, giving the wing a slightly hooked appearance. Very little is known about this moth.

5159 - *Desmia funeralis*
Grape Leaffolder Moth

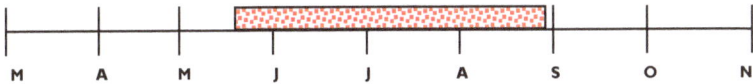

Host: Grape and Virginia creeper.

Range: Ohio River Valley and Lower Great Lakes.

Habitat: A variety of open and wooded habitats.

Identification: The three obvious white spots on each side make this bug obvious. There is also a pair of white stripes on the abdomen. This is a very common moth in wooded areas.

5226 - *Palpita magniferalis*
Splendid Palpita Moth

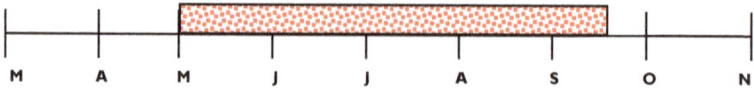

M	A	M	J	J	A	S	O	N

Host: Ash.

Range: Throughout the Midwest.

Habitat: A variety of habitats including wetlands, open fields, and woodland edges and openings.

Identification: The quantity and size of the dark markings on this moth can vary widely, as indicated by the moth to the right.

5292 - *Conchylodes ovulalis*
Zebra Conchylodes Moth

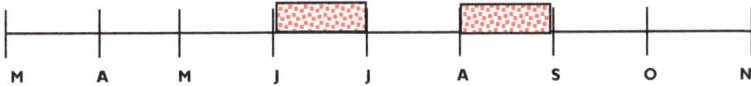

Host: Several members of the Sunflower Family.

Range: Ohio River Valley.

Habitat: Fields and woodland edges.

Identification: The bold black striping on the white background in unmistakable. Also the black and yellow striping on the abdomen is unique. Data suggests two distinct generations during the season. Always a fun find!

5464 - *Urola nivalis*
Snowy Urola Moth

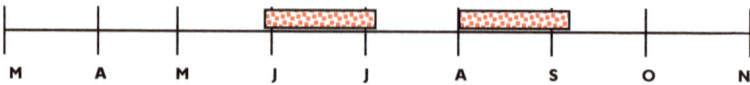

Host: Grasses.

Range: Throughout the Midwest.

Habitat: All habitats that include native grasses.

Identification: This moth has satiny white wings with a gold fringe on the forewings and a slight dark spot on top of the folded wings. This moth is easily recognized among our micromoths.

6091 - *Geina periscelidactylus*
Grape Plume Moth

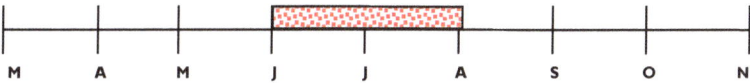

Host: Grape and Virginia creeper.

Range: Ohio River Valley and Lower Great Lakes.

Habitat: Primarily woodland edges.

Identification: There are several plume moths found in the Midwest. The grape plume is the most easily recognized by the brown band (white arrow) on the tan base-colored forewings. The Plume Moths are easily recognized by the narrow perpendicular wings with spiny, thin legs. These moths are frequently found on flowers, especially milkweed, during the day.

6251 - *Drepana arcuata*
Arched Hooktip Moth

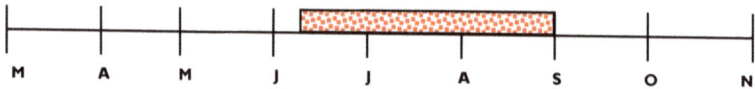

Host: Alder and birch.

Range: Throughout the Midwest.

Habitat: A variety of habitats, sometimes at considerable distance from the host plant.

Identification: The hooked wing tips (black arrow) are a dead giveaway for this moth. This moth is not especially common, making it a fun find at any sheet.

6261 - *Heliomata cycladata*
Common Spring Moth

Host: Black locust and honeylocust.

Range: Ohio River Valley and Lower Great Lakes.

Habitat: Woodland edges and openings.

Identification: The large white hindwing spot is unlike any other small moth that we have. These moths can be found both day and night.

6273 - *Speranza pustularia*
Lesser Maple Spanworm Moth

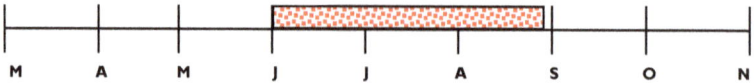

M   A   M   J   J   A   S   O   N

Host: Maple, birch, and cherry.

Range: Throughout the Midwest.

Habitat: A variety of habitats ranging from open fields and wetlands to forest edges and openings.

Identification: The plain white background with cinnamon-colored narrow stripes is unique among our summer moths. This moth can be seasonally abundant, with several dozen showing up to a sheet in a single night.

6599 - *Epimecis hortaria*
Tuliptree Beauty Moth

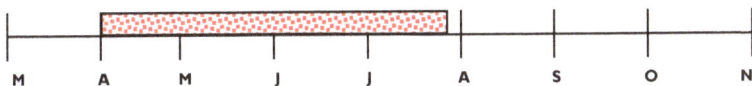

Host: Tuliptree, pawpaw, sassafras, and poplar.

Range: The Ohio River Valley.

Habitat: A variety of habitats. The key is to have host tree species nearby.

Identification: The Tuliptree Beauty resembles many of the other gray geometrid (inchworm) moths. The distinguishing difference is this moth's size, with a wingspan which easily reaches two inches, double the width of most geometrids.

6640 - *Biston betularia*
Peppered Moth

M — A — M — J — J — A — S — O — N

Host: A wide variety of plants.

Range: Throughout the Midwest.

Habitat: Woodland edges and fields.

Identification: This moth is sort of a salt and pepper color with dark veins in the forewing. Another unique characteristic about the Peppered Moth is the way it holds its wings. The forewings are held lower, nearly completely concealing the hindwings. This moth frequently has a white face. Data suggests two distinct generations for this moth.

6740 - *Xanthotype urticaria*
False Crocus Geometer Moth

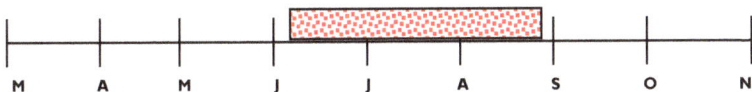

M   A   M   J   J   A   S   O   N

Host: Dogwood and goldenrod.

Range: Throughout the Midwest.

Habitat: Open fields and woodland edges.

Identification: The yellow wings with red blotches is quite unique among geometers. There is also a Crocus Geometer which looks very similar and some scientists consider the two to be the same species.

6818 - *Selenia kentaria*
Kent's Geometer

Host: Cherry and birch.
Range: Ohio River Valley.
Habitat: Woodland edges and openings.
Identification: Your mind will try to convince you this is a butterfly rather than a moth. This moth frequently folds it's wings over its back, much like a butterfly. The combination of oranges, browns, and frosting gives this moth a breathtaking appearance. Look for the silver comma (white arrow) to confirm the identification. Consider finding this moth as a real treat!

6838 - *Probole amicaria*
Friendly Probole Moth

Host: Sourwood.

Range: Ohio River Valley.

Habitat: Woodland edges.

Identification: There are several relatively large speckled geometers. The friendly probole is recognized by the large tooth that sometimes extends nearly to the wing margin (white arrow). I can find no references as to what about this moth is "friendly".

6840 - *Plagodis serinaria*
Lemon Plagodis Moth

M   A   M   J   J   A   S   O   N

Host: Poplar, birch, and cherry.
Range: Ohio River Valley
Habitat: Woodland edges and openings.
Identification: The *Plagodis* are a beautiful group of moths with interesting wing shapes and wonderful color patterns and designs. The Lemon Plagodis is lemon yellow with a burgundy blush. A beautiful moth!

6841 - *Plagodis kuetzingi*
Purple Plagodis Moth

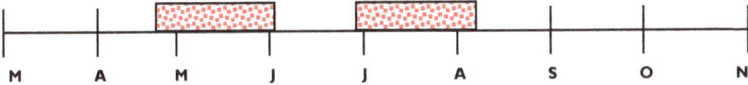

Host: Ash.

Range: Ohio and Mississippi River Valleys.

Habitat: Open areas with nearby host plants.

Identification: The *Plagodis* are a beautiful group of moths with interesting wing shapes and wonderful color patterns and designs. The apical half of all wings of this species are dark purple with the basal half being brown, and in some cases, approaching a woodgrain appearance. A special find at any sheet!

6843 - *Plagodis fervidaria*
Fervid Plagodis Moth

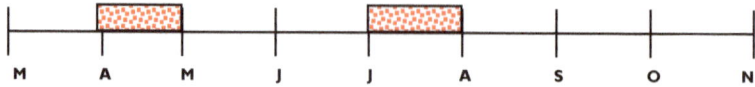

Host: Several deciduous tree species.
Range: Ohio and Mississippi River Valleys.
Habitat: Woodland edges and openings.
Identification: The *Plagodis* are a beautiful group of moths with interesting wing shapes and wonderful color patterns and designs. This moth is striking with its woodgrain appearance. The horizontal line on the forewings (white arrow) is not always present.

66

6982 - *Prochoerodes transversata*
Large Maple Spanworm Moth

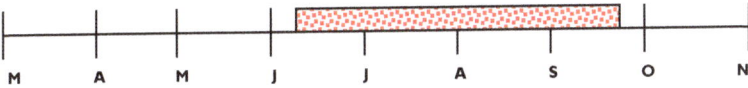

Host: Maple and several other deciduous trees.

Range: Throughout the Midwest.

Habitat: A wide variety of habitats.

Identification: This moth can be quite variable in its color and markings. The wood burned "squigglies" (white arrow) on the hindwing are not always present. The other lines are fairly consistent, although vary in their boldness.

7053 - *Dichorda iridaria*
Showy Emerald Moth

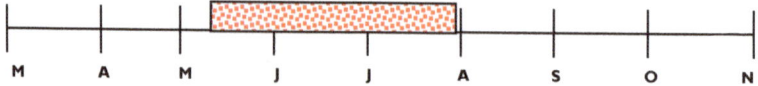

M	A	M	J	J	A	S	O	N

Host: Sumac and poison ivy.

Range: Ohio River Valley.

Habitat: Wherever the host plants are found.

Identification: Notice that the forewings have two white lines while the hindwings have but one. This moth also has a white frosting throughout. Also notice the dark leading edge of the forewing near the head (white arrow). These are the features that make the boldly marked Showy Emerald unique among the emeralds.

7146 - *Haematopis grataria*
Chickweed Geometer

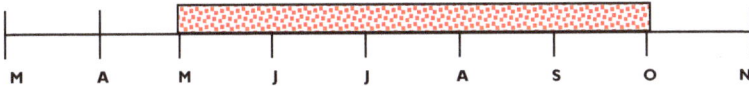

Host: Chickweed and clover.
Range: Throughout the Midwest.
Habitat: Gardens, lawns, and fields.
Identification: The pink lines and edging is unique among our Midwestern moths. You are far more likely to find this moth during the daytime fluttering through the grass than coming to a sheet at night.

7159 - *Scopula limboundata*
Large Lace-border Moth

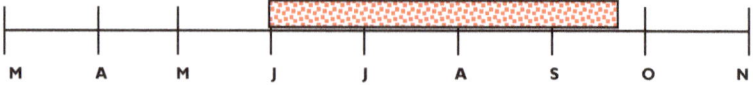

M	A	M	J	J	A	S	O	N

Host: Cherry, apple, clover, blueberry, and dandelion.

Range: Throughout the Midwest.

Habitat: A variety of habitats.

Identification: The Lace-border Moth is the typical geometrid shape. The amount of dark spotting on the wings can vary greatly, from no spots at all to nearly completely covered in spots. This species is a regular at Midwestern sheets and sometimes are quite abundant.

7181 - *Lophosis labeculata*
Stained Lophosis Moth

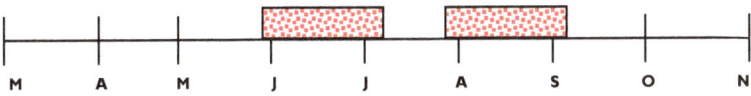

Host: Unknown.
Range: Ohio River Valley.
Habitat: Fields and open areas.
Identification: The Stained Lophosis is sexually dimorphic, meaning male and female appear very differently. Pictured above is a female. The male only has yellow along the wing margins (right). Otherwise, very little is known about this unique little moth.

7196 - *Eulithis diversilineata*
Lesser Grapevine Looper Moth

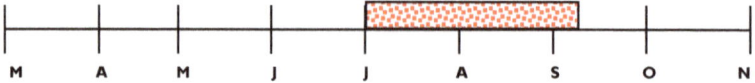

Host: Virginia creeper and grape.

Range: Ohio and Mississippi River Valleys.

Habitat: A variety of habitats but a preference for open fields.

Identification: Note the multiple, alternating bands with a tooth (white arrow) that extends into a frosted area nearly to the wing edge. There is also a Greater Grapevine Looper which looks identical to this moth, just slightly larger. This moth tends to hold its abdomen in odd positions, in this case over the top of its head.

7214 - *Gandaritis atricolorata*
Dark-banded Geometer Moth

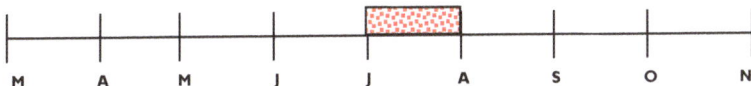

| M | A | M | J | J | A | S | O | N |

Host: Unknown.
Range: Ohio River Valley.
Habitat: Unknown.
Identification: Very little is known about this moth. The dark base color with the boldly contrasting silver-yellow lines is unlike anything else, making the identification of this moth super easy.

7292 - *Rheumaptera prunivorata*
Ferguson's Scallop Shell Moth

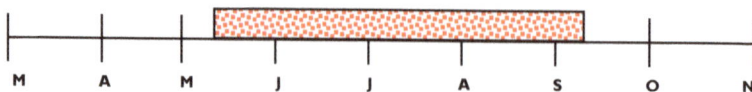

M	A	M	J	J	A	S	O	N

Host: Cherry.

Range: Ohio River Valley and Lower Great Lakes.

Habitat: A variety of habitats.

Identification: Perhaps the easiest of our moths to identify with its numerous, tightly packed, squiggly, parallel lines. Fresh specimens are quite striking.

7440 - *Eubaphe mendica*
Beggar Moth

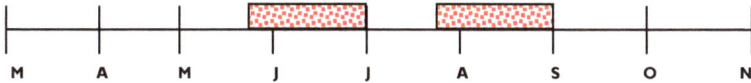

Host: Maple and violets.

Range: Throughout the Midwest.

Habitat: A variety of habitats.

Identification: The pastel yellow (nearly translucent) with the pale purple spots is very unique among Midwestern moths. The wing shape is also very unusual for a member of the geometrid (inchworm) moths in that it completely lacks any scalloping at all on the wing margins.

7648 - *Dyspteris abortivaria*
Badwing Moth

M | A | M | J | J | A | S | O | N

Host: Grape and Virginia creeper.
Range: Ohio River Valley and Lower Great Lakes.
Habitat: Woodland edges and openings.
Identification: This moth looks like it should be in the emerald group but it is not. The hindwings are MUCH smaller than the forewings, which makes it very different from the emeralds, and is the source for the common name.

7663 - *Apatelodes torrefacta*
Spotted Apatelodes Moth

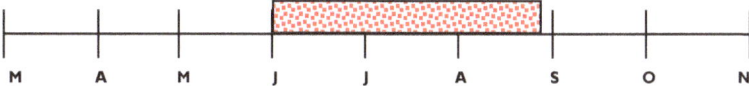

| M | | A | | M | | J | | J | | A | | S | | O | | N |

Host: Cherry, ash, maple, and oak.
Range: Ohio River Valley and Lower Great Lakes.
Habitat: A variety of habitats with nearby host plants.
Identification: This is one of our most recognizable moths, with the hindwings held beneath the forewings, exposing the complete abdomen. It also has prominent dark spots on the inner part of the forewing (white arrow), and prominent white spots toward the apex of the forewing (black arrow). Caterpillar (right).

7670 - *Tolype velleda*
Large Tolype Moth

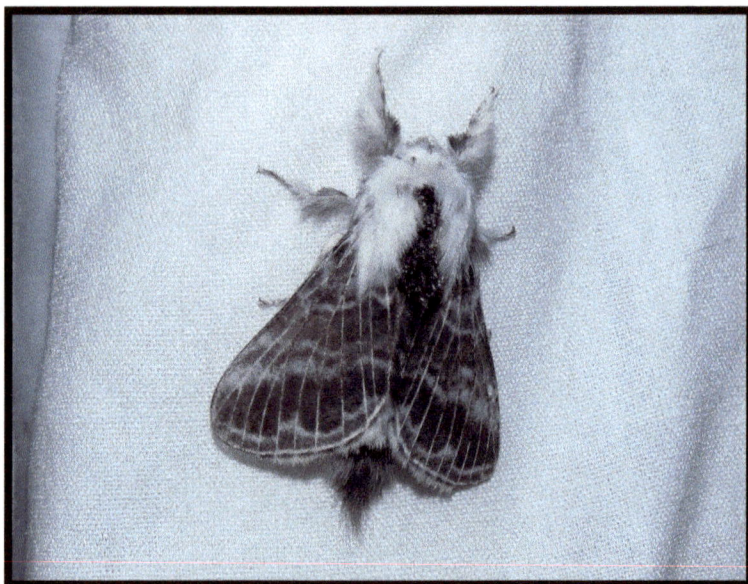

| M | A | M | J | J | A | S | O | N |

Host: Several deciduous tree and shrub species.
Range: Throughout the Midwest.
Habitat: A variety of habitats.
Identification: This late season moth is easily recognized by the dingy gray wings contrasting with white veins. The white, furry head and thorax are very obvious and the abdomen sticks out beyond the wings.

7683 - *Artace cribrarius*
Dot-lined White Moth

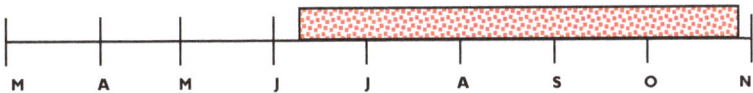

Host: Oak, cherry, and rose.

Host: Oak, cherry, and rose.
Range: Ohio River Valley.
Habitat: A variety of habitats.
Identification: This moth is easily recognized by the black dots on white wings that form a linear arrangement. Also note the golden-colored antennae on the white head. The abdomen tends to be extended well beyond the wings. This moth has two distinct seasons; mid-summer and again in mid-autumn.

7704 - *Eacles imperialis*
Imperial Moth

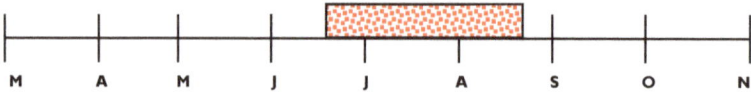

M   A   M   J   J   A   S   O   N

Host: Several deciduous tree and shrub species.

Range: Throughout the Midwest.

Habitat: Despite hosting on largely forest tree species, Imperials more frequently come to sheets in open areas.

Identification: The Imperial Moth's markings can vary. Males are normally more heavily marked than females (female above, male right). Generally look for red/purple blotching on a yellow background. These moths do NOT feed as adults, therefore cannot be considered pollinators.

7706 - *Citheronia regalis*
Regal Moth

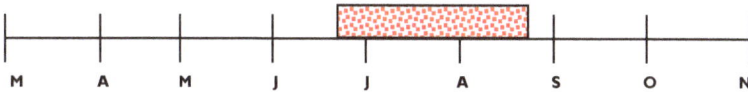

M	A	M	J	J	A	S	O	N

Host: Several deciduous tree species.

Range: Ohio River Valley and Lower Great Lakes.

Habitat: Despite hosting on largely forest tree species, Regals more frequently come to sheets in open areas.

Identification: This moth has a very unique appearance with a gray/brown base color, red wing veins, and yellow speckles. This moth also goes by the name Royal Walnut Moth. The caterpillar is known as a Hickory Horned Devil because of its fearsome appearance (right).

81

7715 - *Dryocampa rubicunda*
Rosy Maple Moth

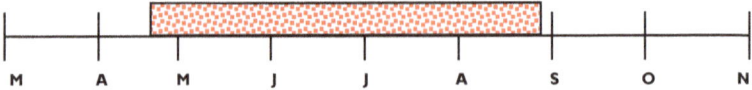

M	A	M	J	J	A	S	O	N

Host: Maple, beech, oak, and sycamore.

Range: Ohio and Mississippi River Valleys.

Habitat: A variety of habitats.

Identification: The combination of pink and yellow is unlike anything else that flies in the Midwest with the exception of the Pink Prominent moth. The Pink Prominent, however has a pink body rather than yellow. The Rosy Maple Moth is one of the most frequently encountered members of the Giant Silkmoth family.

7746 - *Automeris io*
Io Moth

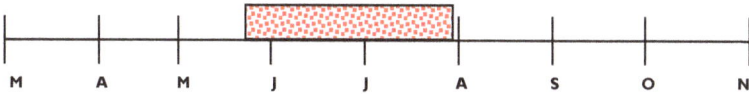

| M | A | M | J | J | A | S | O | N |

Host: A wide variety of tree species.

Range: Throughout the Midwest.

Habitat: Despite hosting on largely forest tree species, Ios more frequently come to sheets in open areas.

Identification: This moth is easily recognized by the large eyespots and red blush on the hindwings. The forewings of the Io Moth slightly resemble those of the Imperial Moth, but the Io is typically smaller. The Io is sexually dimorphic with the male being yellow and the female more of a reddish-tan color. The spines on the caterpillar yield a painful sting to the person who touches them.

7757 - *Antheraea polyphemus*
Polyphemus Moth

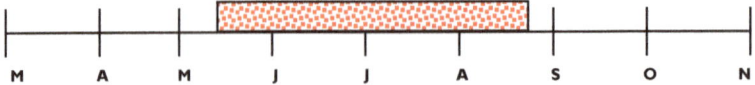

Host: Oak, birch, maple, hickory, and grape.

Range: Throughout the Midwest.

Habitat: Despite hosting on largely forest tree species, Polyphemus' more frequently come to sheets in open areas.

Identification: The Polyphemus is easily recognized by the pink brackets (white arrows) on the inner part of the forewing as well as the single eyespot on each wing. It also has a single eyespot on each hindwing, however these spots are normally concealed by the forewings.

7758 - *Actias luna*
Luna Moth

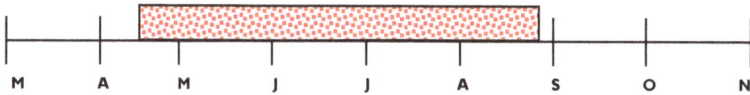

| M | | A | | M | | J | | J | | A | | S | | O | | N |

Host: Hickory, walnut, sumac, and other tree species
Range: Throughout the Midwest.
Habitat: A variety of habitats.
Identification: With its green color and long tails, the Luna Moth is probably the most recognized moth in the United States, including having its own television commercial (Lunesta)! This is a special visitor to any sheet or porch light. Caterpillar (right).

7767 - *Hyalophora cecropia*
Cecropia Moth

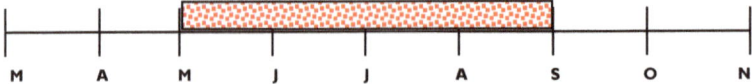

M A M J J A S O N

Host: Many deciduous tree species, but prefers ash.
Range: Throughout the Midwest.
Habitat: A variety of habitats.
Identification: The Cecropia is easily distinguished from the Promethea and Tulip Tree Moths by the broad red band and large white spot on the hindwings viewable from both sides of the wings. Throughout the Midwest, Cecropia numbers are said to be in decline, largely due to habitat loss from urbanization and agriculture. Caterpillar (right).

7809 - *Sphinx kalmiae*
Laurel Sphinx Moth

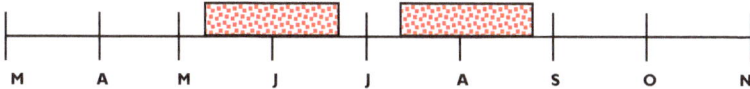

M	A	M	J	J	A	S	O	N

Host: Ash, lilac, and privet
Range: Throughout the Midwest.
Habitat: Fields, yards, and woodland openings.
Identification: One of the easiest to identify sphinx moths because of the woodgrain appearance of the forewings. The name is very misleading. This moth is actually named after early botanist Peter Kalm, NOT after the scientific name of Mountain Laurel.

7825 - *Paonias myops*
Small-eyed Sphinx Moth

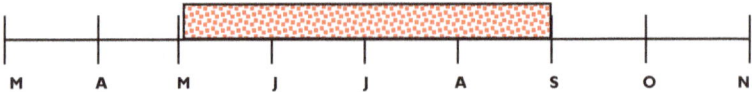

Host: Birch, poplar, cherry, and willow.

Range: Ohio and Mississippi River Valleys.

Habitat: Fields and woodland openings and edges.

Identification: Notice the pair of gray stripes (white arrows) on the back of the head and thorax rather than the violin design of the similar Blind-eyed Sphinx. In addition, Small-eyed Sphinx has much more yellow (yellow arrows) in the wings.

7853 - *Hemaris thysbe*
Hummingbird Clearwing Moth

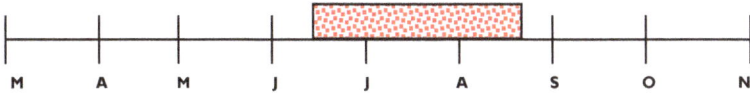

Host: Honeysuckle, viburnum, and snowberry.

Range: Throughout the Midwest.

Habitat: Open fields and gardens.

Identification: The term 'Hummingbird Moth' typically refers to Sphinx Moths which fly during the day and hover over flowers as they imbibe nectar, thus appearing at a distance to be a hummingbird. Many of these 'Hummingbird Moths' have translucent wings. This moth is recognized by the maroon and olive-tan color. These moths love to nectar on Bergamot (*Monarda fistulosa*).

7855 - *Hemaris diffinis*
Snowberry Clearwing Moth

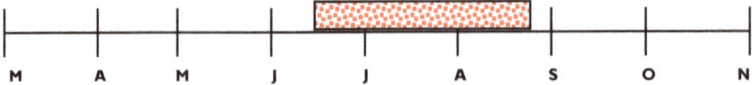

M	A	M	J	J	A	S	O	N

Host: Honeysuckle and snowberry.
Range: Throughout the Midwest.
Habitat: Open fields and gardens.
Identification: The term 'Hummingbird Moth' typically refers to Sphinx Moths which fly during the day and hover over flowers as they imbibe nectar, thus appearing at a distance to be a hummingbird. This moth has a black -yellow color pattern, very much resembling a bumble bee!

7859 - *Eumorpha pandorus*
Pandorus Sphinx Moth

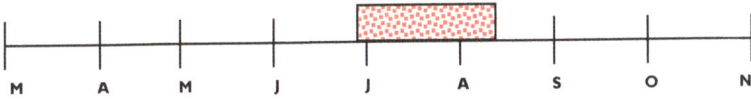

M   A   M   J   J   A   S   O   N

Host: Grape and Virginia creeper.

Range: Throughout the Midwest.

Habitat: Despite hosting on largely forest vine species, Pandorus more frequently come to sheets in open areas.

Identification: The green mottled color of Pandorus Sphinx is not only beautiful but also unique. The only other moth with a similar pattern is the Virginia Creeper Sphinx which is sort of a miniature version of Pandorus.

7870 - *Sphecodina abbottii*
Abbott's Sphinx Moth

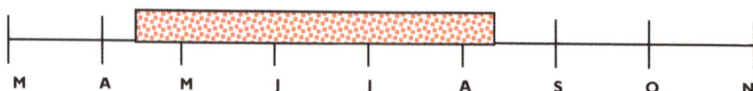

M   A   M   J   J   A   S   O   N

Host: Grape.

Range: Throughout the Midwest.

Habitat: Open areas and woodland edges.

Identification: A fresh Abbott's Sphinx has a beautiful wood grain look. But even worn individuals will have the bright yellow hindwing and the tuft of yellow hairs on the abdomen (white arrows). While seasonal data indicates that they fly into August, this moth is much more common in spring. Early instar caterpillar (right).

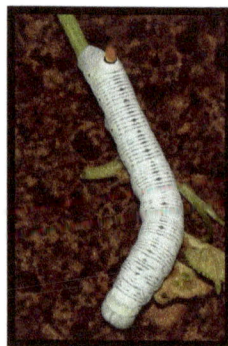

7873 - *Amphion floridensis*
Nessus Sphinx Moth

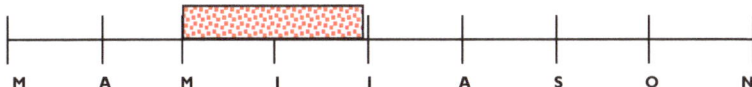

M   A   M   J   J   A   S   O   N

Host: Grape.

Range: Throughout the Midwest.

Habitat: Open areas with nectar resources.

Identification: Nessus Sphinx is a bee mimic, with brightly colored stripes on a dark body. This moth hovers above the flowers from which it is drinking nectar, much like a hummingbird. You are not likely to see this one during the night but rather in the daytime.

7885 - *Darapsa myron*
Virginia Creeper Sphinx Moth

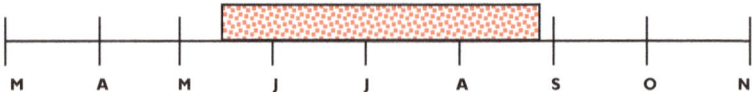

Host: Grape and Virginia creeper.

Range: Throughout the Midwest.

Habitat: Despite hosting on largely forest vine species, these moths more frequently come to sheets in open areas.

Identification: While the same general color scheme as Pandorus Sphinx, Virginia Creeper Sphinx has thick color bands; Pandorus is more of a mosaic of color, almost like a checkerboard. Pandorus Sphinx is also the much larger of the two.

7890 - *Xylophanes tersa*
Tersa Sphinx Moth

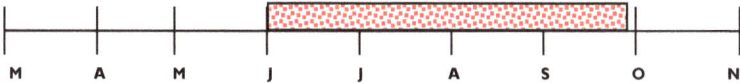

| M | A | M | J | J | A | S | O | N |

Host: Catalpa and possibly buttonbush.
Range: Throughout the Midwest.
Habitat: Open areas with nearby host plants.
Identification: This moth has to be considered one of the most beautiful in the Midwest, with a woodgrain appearance and sleek, crisp lines and features. A definite show-stopper! These mimic hummingbirds with their daytime, hovering feeding style.

7915 - *Nadata gibbosa*
White-dotted Prominent Moth

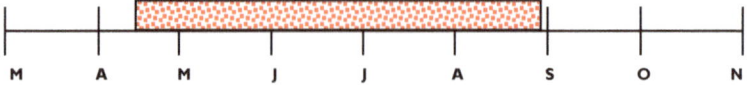

| M | | A | | M | | J | | J | | A | | S | | O | | N |

Host: Oak, beech, and other deciduous tree species.

Range: Throughout the Midwest.

Habitat: A variety of habitats.

Identification: Look for one or two very small white dots (white arrow) on the yellow/brown forewing, placed halfway between the two red lines. This species also tends to have a yellow top-knot on its head (black arrow).

7921 - *Peridea ferruginea*
Chocolate Prominent Moth

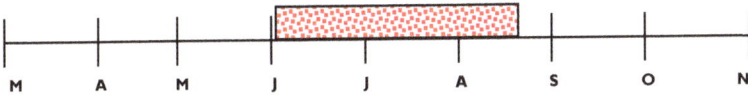

Host: Birch.

Range: Throughout the Midwest.

Habitat: Despite hosting on largely forest tree species, these moths more frequently come to sheets in open areas.

Identification: The chocolate brown mask (white arrow) on the otherwise gray wings is a good identification tool for this moth. Usually there is also some brown near the head. While this moth may have a broad range, it in no way should be considered common or abundant.

7936 - *Furcula borealis*
White Fercula Moth

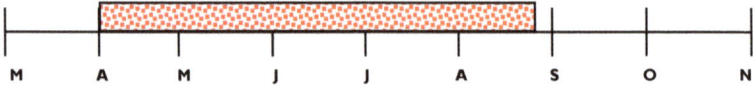

Host: Cherry, willow, and poplar.

Range: Throughout the Midwest.

Habitat: A variety of habitats.

Identification: This moth is easily identified by the dark mask on the white background of the forewings. Some people say there is a monkey face (white arrow) on the back of the thorax. I think it looks more like a pug face! While this moth has a broad range, it is not especially abundant.

7937 - *Furcula cinerea*
Gray Fercula Moth

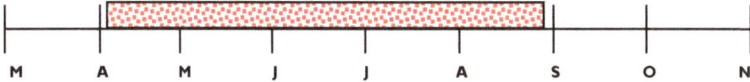

Host: Birch, willow, and poplar.

Range: Throughout the Midwest.

Habitat: A variety of habitats.

Identification: This moth is beautifully unique with its gray base color with yellow-orange spots. In my experience, this species is not as common as its cousin the White Furcula. This is indeed is a special find at any sheet!

8022 - *Hyparpax aurora*
Pink Prominent Moth

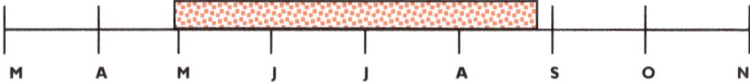

M	A	M	J	J	A	S	O	N

Host: Oak and viburnum.
Range: Throughout the Midwest.
Habitat: Unknown.
Identification: This is a special moth indeed! Pink Prominent is rarely seen at sheets. The question begs, is the Pink Prominent rare, or does it rarely come to lights at night? We need more sightings, of both adults and larva, to make this determination. This moth superficially, but strongly, resembles Rosy Maple Moth, so care needs to be taken to not confuse the two. The easiest distinction is that Rosy Maple has a yellow body, Pink Prominent a pink body.

8067 - *Cisthene plumbea*
Lead-colored Lichen Moth

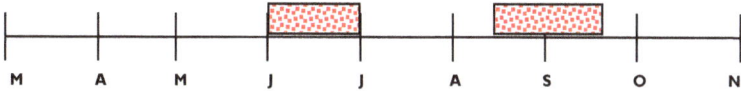

Host: Lichen.
Range: Ohio River Valley.
Habitat: A variety of habitats.
Identification: The forewings of this species are a dingy gray framed by pastel yellow. The hindwings are salmon-colored. The Lead-colored Lichen Moth has two distinct broods, hence the break in the timeline above. The late-summer brood seems to have a larger population then the early brood.

8089 - *Hypoprepia miniata*
Scarlet-winged Lichen Moth

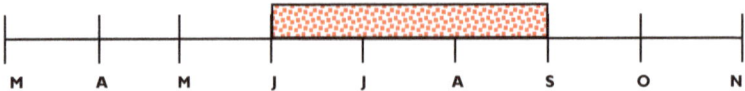

| M | | A | | M | | J | | J | | A | | S | | O | | N |

Host: Lichen.
Range: Ohio and Mississippi River Valleys.
Habitat: A variety of habitats.
Identification: The bright red wings cannot be confused with anything else! Research indicates these moths prefer lichens associated with pine forests.

8090 - *Hypoprepia fucosa*
Painted Lichen Moth

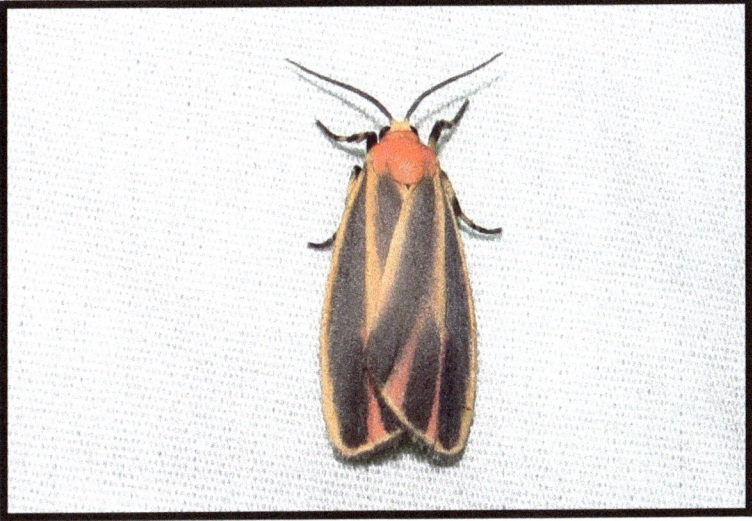

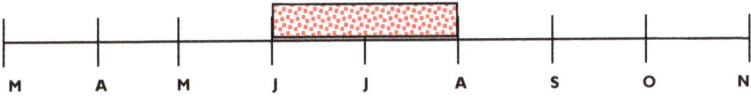

M | A | M | J | J | A | S | O | N

Host: Lichen and moss.

Range: Throughout the Midwest.

Habitat: Woodland openings and edges.

Identification: The blending of bright yellow and red is unique among our moths, and makes for a very beautiful combination. The caterpillars of this species feed primarily on lichens and mosses found on the sides of trees. A wonderful addition to any sheet!

8107 - *Haploa clymene*
Clymene Moth

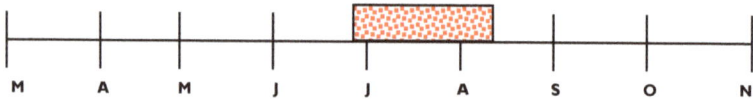

Host: Oak, willow, snakeroot, boneset, and Joe pye weed.
Range: Ohio River Valley and Lower Great Lakes.
Habitat: Open fields and wetlands.
Identification: When the forewings are held together, the dark pattern looks sort of like an angel. The hindwings are a golden yellow. The Clymene Moth is frequently found during the day as well, usually among grasses and wildflowers.

8129 - *Pyrrharctia isabella*
Isabella Tiger Moth

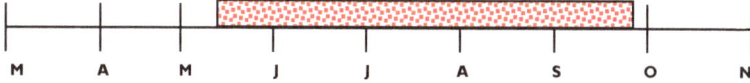

Host: A wide variety of plants.

Range: Throughout the Midwest.

Habitat: A variety of habitats.

Identification: Forewings are golden with a few black spots. Hindwings are a pale yellow. Abdomen is yellow with black spots. The caterpillar for this species is the Wooly Bear, the official winter weather predicting caterpillar. It is believed the Isabella Tiger Moth caterpillar is nearly as accurate with their predictions as the meteorologists!.

8146 - *Hypercompe scribonia*
Giant Leopard Moth

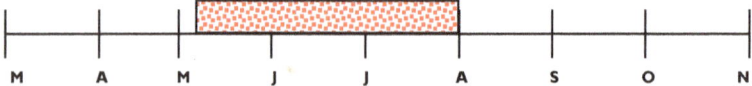

```
├─────┼─────┼─████████████████████┼─────┼─────┼─────┼─────┤
  M     A     M     J     J     A     S     O     N
```

Host: Many species of plants.
Range: Throughout the Midwest.
Habitat: A variety of habitats but seems to prefer open areas.
Identification: The large black spots on the white background is very unique, with some of the spots filled with a brilliant blue. The legs and antennae are also blue. This is the largest of our tiger moths. The caterpillar looks very similar to the Wooly Bear, the name given to the larva of the Isabella Tiger Moth.

8211 - *Lophocampa caryae*
Hickory Tussock Moth

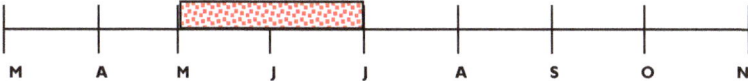

| M | A | M | J | J | A | S | O | N |

Host: Hickory and several other deciduous tree species.
Range: Eastern portions of the Midwest.
Habitat: Woodland edges.
Identification: A beautiful moth with golden-brown base color and large cream-colored spots. In portions of the range, these moths are very abundant and will appear by the hundreds on mothing sheets.

8230 - *Cycnia tenera*
Delicate Cycnia Moth

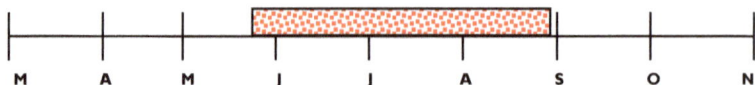

| M | A | M | J | J | A | S | O | N |

Host: Milkweed and dogbane.

Range: Throughout the Midwest.

Habitat: Open fields and woodland edges.

Identification: The white forewings with a lemon yellow leading edge is very unique among our moths. The caterpillar has long gray hairs and can be frequently found on milkweed, especially Butterfly Weed.

8397 - *Palthis angulalis*
Dark-spotted Palthis Moth

M	A	M	J	J	A	S	O	N

Host: A wide variety of deciduous and evergreen trees.

Range: Throughout the Midwest.

Habitat: A variety of habitats.

Identification: In the Dark-spotted Palthis, the middle dark band is not straight but points to the head (white arrow). The black arrow indicates the dark spot mentioned in the name. In the very similar Faint-spotted Palthis, the dark band is straight (inset photo). The shape of both of these moths is very unique.

8528 - *Hypsoropha hormos*
Small Necklace Moth

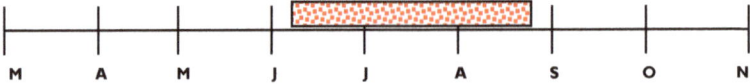

M	A	M	J	J	A	S	O	N

Host: Persimmon and sassafras.

Range: Ohio River Valley.

Habitat: Open fields and woodland edges.

Identification: While the base color of this moth can vary, those white pearly spots across the top are unmistakable. This is a special find at any sheet!

8649 - *Ascalapha odorata*
Black Witch Moth

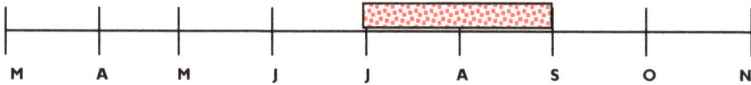

Host: Do not reproduce in the Midwest.

Range: The Deep South and desert Southwest.

Habitat: Random.

Identification: The Black Witch is strictly a random migrant from Mexico and the Southwest. While there have been sightings in all Midwestern states, those sightings have been sparse. If one of these lands on your sheet, you will know it, believing initially it is a bat. The Black Witch has a wingspan of nearly six inches. The colors in the different bands and eyespots on the wings are simply breathtaking. The photo above was taken in Arizona.

8717 - *Zale horrida*
Horrid Zale

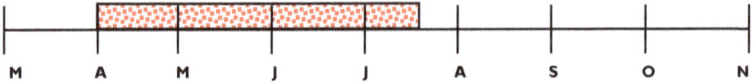

M	A	M	J	J	A	S	O	N

Host: Viburnum.

Range: Ohio River Valley and Lower Great Lakes.

Habitat: Woodland edges and openings.

Identification: The Zale group is very large but largely do not have real distinctive features, except for this one. The two distinct, contrasting colors bands are very unique. In addition, this moth frequently has an obvious ruffled collar, which is not only unique to the Zales but to all moths.

112

8890 - *Chrysodeixis includens*
Soybean Looper Moth

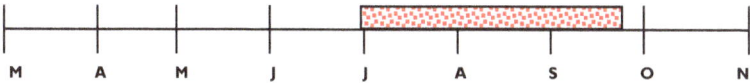

```
|----+----+----+----+----+::::::::::::::::::+----+----|
M    A    M    J    J    A    S    O    N
```

Host: Soybeans and other agricultural crops.

Range: Throughout the Midwest.

Habitat: Woodland edges and openings.

Identification: This is a very unique moth with what appears to be gold leaf or gold plating on the wings. Because of this moth's status as an agricultural pest there will always be a degree of warfare against it. A lovely find on any sheet, unless you are a soybean grower.

8957 - *Paectes oculatrix*
Eyed Paectes Moth

| | | | | | | | | |
|M|A|M|J|J|A|S|O|N|

Host: Poison ivy.

Range: Throughout the Midwest.

Habitat: Open areas and woodland edges.

Identification: The large eyespots at the forewing tips are very unique among our Midwestern moths. There is also a pale patch at the base of the forewing to help confirm your identification. The fact that this moth hosts on poison ivy makes it very popular at our house. No, you will not get poison ivy if this moth lands on you!

9025 - *Oruza albocostaliata*
White Edge Moth

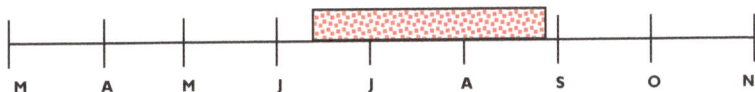

| M | A | M | J | J | A | S | O | N |

Host: Unknown.
Range: Ohio River Valley.
Habitat: Open fields and woodland edges.
Identification: This moth is very recognizable by the white, leading edge of the forewing. The pair of white lines in the wings are reminiscent of some of the emeralds, but this moth is in the Noctuid group of moths while the emeralds are in the Geometrid group. Very little is known about this species.

Black-bordered Lemon Moth

M	A	M	J	J	A	S	O	N

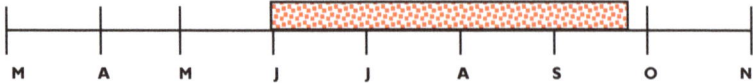

Host: Crabgrass.

Range: Ohio River Valley and Lower Great Lakes.

Habitat: Open fields and woodland edges.

Identification: This moth is small, but not so small to be considered a micromoth. The yellow base color with the black margin is very unique. This moth also has two small black dots on each forewing.

9047 - *Protodeltote muscosula*
Large Mossy Lithacodia Moth

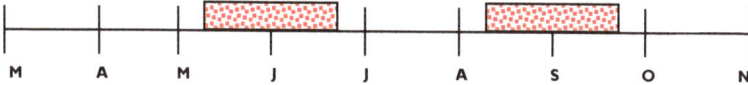

Host: The only listing available is an ambiguous reference to "Swamp Grasses".

Range: Throughout the Midwest.

Habitat: Wetlands and woodland edges.

Identification: A fun little moth; the design on the wings reminds me of an Easter Island head! Black arrow indicates the eyes, yellow arrow cheeks, and white arrow mouth. The only host information available doesn't pass the smell test, as many places where these moths are found are not even remotely close to swamps.

9065 - *Leuconycta diphteroides*
Green Leuconycta Moth

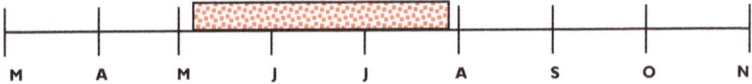

Host: Goldenrod and aster.
Range: Throughout the Midwest.
Habitat: A variety of habitats.
Identification: There are several green owlet moths in the Midwest region. The two dark patches (white arrows) on the leading edge of the forewing is distinctive among these moths. The white markings sort of resemble water droplets.

9177 - *Panthea acronyctoides*
Black Zigzag Moth

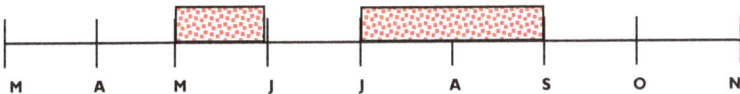

M   A   M   J   J   A   S   O   N

Host: Hemlock and pine.

Range: Western Appalachian foothills.

Habitat: Despite hosting on largely forest tree species, Zigzags more frequently come to sheets in open areas.

Identification: Zigzag is an appropriate description for the black lines that run horizontally across the white forewings. Black and white moths are few and far between anyways, but the zigzag black lines on the white background is very unique. A fun find at any sheet!

9182 - *Panthea furcilla*
Eastern Panthea Moth

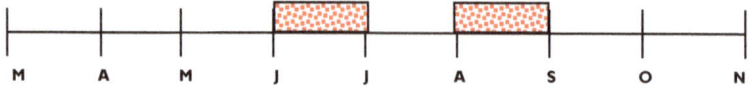

M   A   M   J   J   A   S   O   N

Host: Pine.
Range: Western Appalachians and Great Lakes.
Habitat: Woodland edges and openings.
Identification: This species is similar to the Zigzag but the lines are straighter and the base color is gray rather than white. This species has two generations each year. Limited to areas with large acreage of conifers.

9221 - *Acronicta funeralis*
Funerary Dagger Moth

Host: A wide variety of deciduous trees.

Range: Throughout the Midwest and especially in the Ohio River Valley.

Habitat: A variety of habitats.

Identification: There are many different species of dagger moths, and the Funerary is among the most unique and beautiful. The inside margins of the forewings are dark shaded, creating a long dark rectangle when the wings are closed. Also note the dark triangle near the reniform spot (white arrow).

9241 - *Acronicta fragilis*
Fragile Dagger Moth

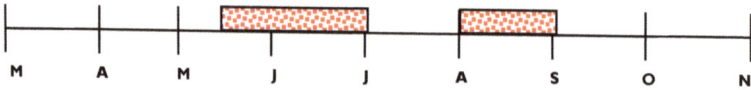

Host: Apple, birch, plum, willow, and spruce.
Range: Appalachian foothills and Upper Great Lakes.
Habitat: A variety of habitats.
Identification: This moth has a showy display of zigzag black lines on a white background. On the back of the thorax is a design that could be easily recognized as a skull face (red circle).

9281 - *Acronicta fallax*
Green Marvel

Host: Viburnum.

Range: Throughout the Midwest.

Habitat: Woodland edges and openings.

Identification: While there are several different green moths in the Midwest, this one is unique. This moth is easily recognized by the green base color with black chevrons scattered throughout the forewings. The shade of green, to the artistic eye is slightly different than the others; the Green Marvel has more of a yellow-green whereas many of the others are a blue-green.

9285 - *Polygrammate hebraeicum*
The Hebrew

| M | A | M | J | J | A | S | O | N |

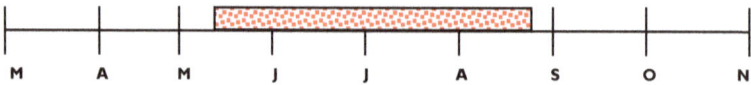

Host: Black Gum.

Range: Ohio River Valley.

Habitat: A variety of habitats.

Identification: The black and white pattern on the forewings is very distinctive. Closest in resemblance would be the Black Zigzag Moth, but notice that the Hebrew's marks are not connected to form a line. Apparently somebody in past thought the marks looked like Hebrew text, hence the common name.

9301 - *Eudryas grata*
Beautiful Wood Nymph

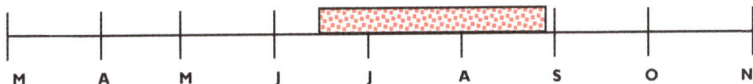

M A M J J A S O N

Host: Grape, hops, and Virginia creeper.
Range: Throughout the Midwest.
Habitat: A variety of habitats.
Identification: The Beautiful Wood Nymph is a fun moth at any sheet. The broad white band bordered in yellow is very unique. The hindwings are gold, but rarely seen. The Pearly Wood Nymph is similar but the yellow border is more subtle and the edge of the white band (white arrow) is smoother (less lumpy).

9309 - *Psychomorpha epimenis*
Grapevine Epimenis Moth

```
|----+----+----+----+----+----+----+----+----|
 M    A    M    J    J    A    S    O    N
```

Host: Grape.

Range: Throughout the Midwest.

Habitat: Open areas especially gravel roads and trails.

Identification: This moth is primarily diurnal or day-flying and it is frequently found puddling on muddy and gravel roads. It has a large white spot on each forewing and a large red/orange spot on each hindwing; a very unique combination.

9314 - *Alypia octomaculata*
Eight-spotted Forester Moth

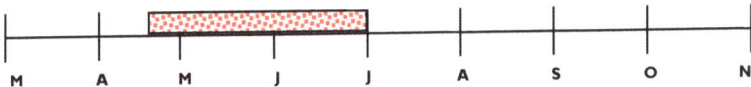

M   A   M   J   J   A   S   O   N

Host: Grape and Virginia creeper.

Range: Throughout the Midwest.

Habitat: Woodland edges and openings.

Identification: This is another largely day-flying moth. Look for two large white spots on each wing plus fuzzy orange legs. While this looks similar to Grape Leaffolder, the Leaffolder lacks the fuzzy orange legs and the white "shoulders".

10891 - *Ochropleura implecta*
Flame-shouldered Dart

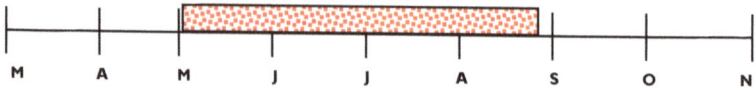

M	A	M	J	J	A	S	O	N

Host: Many herbaceous plants plus willow.
Range: Throughout the Midwest.
Habitat: Woodland edges and openings.
Identification: The prominent cream-colored leading edge of the forewing is a unique feature of this moth, and serves as the flame-shouldered feature of the common name. This species has two generations during the year.

Appendix A

Host Plants of Common and Distinctive Midwestern Moths

Vines

Common Name	Scientific Name	Associated Moth
Grape	*Vitis sp.*	Grape Leaffolder Grape Plume Lesser Grapevine Looper Badwing Pandorus Sphinx Abbott's Sphinx Nessus Sphinx Virginia Creeper Sphinx Beautiful Wood Nymph Grapevine Epimenis Eight-spotted Forester
Honeysuckle	*Lonicera sp.*	Hummingbird Clearwing Snowberry Clearwing
Poison Ivy	*Rhus toxicodendron*	Showy Emerald Eyed Paectes
Virginia Creeper	*Parthenocissus quinquefolia*	Grape Leaffolder Grape Plume Lesser Grapevine Looper Badwing Pandorus Sphinx Virginia Creeper Sphinx Beautiful Wood Nymph Eight-spotted Forester

TREES

Common Name	Scientific Name	Associated Moth
Generalists (Multiple Tree Species)		Carpenterworm Reticulated Fruitworm Tufted Apple Budmoth Black Waved Flannel Skiff Moth Spiny Oak Slug Saddleback Caterpillar Bent-line Gray Canadian Melanolophia Peppered Moth One-spotted Variant White Spring Moth Oak Beauty Pale Beauty Fervid Plagodis Large Maple Spanworm Common Tan Wave Large Tolype Imperial Moth Regal Moth Io Moth Luna Moth Cecropia Moth Banded Tussock Hickory Tussock Dark-spotted Palthis Yellowhorn Moth Funerary Dagger

Common Name	Scientific Name	Associated Moth
Alder	*Alnus sp.*	Arched Hooktip
Apple	*Malus sp.*	Smaller Parasa Large Lace-border
Ash	*Fraxinus sp.*	Splendid Palpita Purple Plagodis Curve-lined Looper Spotted Apatelodes Laurel Sphinx
Basswood	*Linden sp.*	Zigzag Herpetogramma Basswood Leafroller
Beech	*Fagus grandifolia*	Filbertworm Moth Maple Webworm Hollow-spotted Plagodis Rosy Maple White-dotted Prominent Red-lined Panopoda
Birch	*Betula sp.*	Abbreviated Button Slug Yellow-collared Slug Arched Hooktip Lesser Maple Spanworm Kent's Geomeer Lemon Plagodis Polyphemus Moth Small-eyed Sphinx Chocolate Prominent Gray Furcula Maple Looper Unmarked Dagger
Black Gum	*Nyssa sylvatica*	False Underwing The Hebrew

Black Locust	*Robinia pseudoacacia*	Locust Twig Bore Common Spring Locust Underwing
Butternut	*Juglans cinera*	Gray-edged Bomolocha
Catalpa	*Catalpa sp.*	Catalpa Sphinx Tersa Sphinx
Cherry	*Prunus sp.*	Abbreviated Button Slug Lesser Maple Spanworm Kent's Geometer Lemon Plagodis Large Lace-border Spotted Apatelodes Dot-lined White Small-eyed Sphinx White Furcula Unmarked Dagger Speared Dagger
Dogwood	*Cornus florida*	Smaller Parasa False Crocus Geometer
Elm	*Ulmus sp.*	Smaller Parasa White-lined Bomolochaa
Fruit Trees	*Including Peach, Plum, Pear*	Red-banded Leafroller Cherry Agate Speared Dagger
Hemlock	*Tsuga canadensis*	Hemlock Angle Curve-lined Looper Angle-winged Emerald Black Zigzag

Hickory	*Carya sp.*	Yellow-collared Slug Shagreened Slug Polyphemus Moth Brown Panopoda False Underwing Unmarked Dagger Several Underwing species
Honeylocust	*Gleditsia triacanthos*	Common Spring
Hornbeam	*Carpinus sp.* *Ostrya sp.*	Yellow-collared Slug Shagreened Slug
Maple	*Acer sp.*	Maple Callus Borer Abbreviated Button Slug Maple Webworm Common Angle Lesser Maple Spanworm Hollow-spotted Plagodis Beggar Moth Spotted Apatelodes Rosy Maple Polyphemus Moth Baltimore Bomolocha Maple Looper

Oak	*Quercus sp.*	Schlaeger's Fruitworm Filbertworm Moth White-spotted Leafroller Abbreviated Button Slug Yellow-collared Slug Shagreened Slug Spun Glass Slug Smaller Parasa Maple Webworm Oak Webworm Hollow-spotted Plagodis Curve-lined Looper Red-fringed Emerald Spotted Apatelodes Dot-lined White Rosy Maple Polyphemus Moth White-dotted Prominent White-blotched Heterocampa Pink Prominent Faint-spotted Palthis Red-lined Panopoda Brown Panopoda Lunate Zale Speared Dagger
Pawpaw	*Asimina triloba*	Tuliptree Beauty
Persimmon	*Diospyros virginiana*	Small Necklace

Pine	*Pinus sp.*	Granite Moth Black Zigzag Eastern Panthea
Poplar/ Cottonwood	*Populus sp.*	Tuliptree Beauty Lemon Plagoidis Small-eyed Sphinx Common Gluphisia White Furcula Gray Furcula
Sassafras	*Sassafras albidum*	Labyrinth Moth Tuliptree Beauty Small Necklace
Sourwood	*Oxydendrum arboreum*	Friendly Probole
Sumac	*Rhus sp.*	Ailanthus Webworm Showy Emerald Angle-winged Emerald Pygmy Paectes
Sycamore	*Platanus occidentalis*	Rosy Maple
Tree of Heaven	*Ailanthus altissima*	Ailanthus Webworm
Tuliptree	*LIriodendron tulipifera*	Tuliptree Beauty Tuliptree Silkmoth

Walnut	*Juglans nigra*	Gray-edged Bomolocha False Underwing Maple Looper Several Underwing species
Willow	*Salix sp.*	Small-eyed Sphinx White Furcula Gray Furcula Brown Panopoda Unmarked Dagger
Witchhazel	*Hamamelis virginiana*	Labyrinth Moth

Shrubs

Common Name	Scientific Name	Associated Moth
Blackberry	*Rubus sp.*	Ambiguous Moth
Blueberry	*Vaccinium sp.*	Decorated Owlet Large Lace-border
Hazelnut	*Corylus americana*	Filbertworm Moth
Lilac	*Syringa sp.*	Laurel Sphinx
Privet	*Ligusticum sp.*	Laurel Sphinx
Rose	*Rosa sp.*	Dot-lined White Lunate Zale
Snowberry	*Symphoricarpos sp.*	Hummingbird Clearwing Snowberry Clearwing
Viburnum	*Viburnum sp.*	Hummingbird Clearwing Pink Prominent Horrid Zale Green Marvel

Grasses, Forbs, etc

Common Name	Scientific Name	Associated Moth
Multiple Plant Species		Clymene Moth Isabella Tiger Giant Leopard Common Looper Armyworm Flame-shouldered Dart Common Eupithecia
Alfalfa	*Medicago sativa*	Green Cloverworm
Agricultural Crops		Soybean Looper
Aster	*Eurybia sp.* *Machaeranthera sp.* *Symphyotrichum sp.*	Cream-edged Dichomeris Green Leuconycta Ambiguous Moth
Beggar-ticks	*Bidens sp.*	Faint-spotted Palthis
Chickweed	*Cerastium sp.*	Chickweed Geometer
Clover	*Trifolium sp.*	Harnessed Tiger Green Cloverworm Chickweed Geometer
Crabgrass	*Digitaria sp.*	Texas Mocis Black Bordered Lemon
Dandelion	*Taraxacum officinale*	Harnessed Tiger

Dogbane	*Apocynum sp.*	Delicate Cycnia
False Indigo	*Baptisia sp.*	Solidago Root Moth
Fungus		Rotund Idia
Garden Vegetables		Celery Leaftier
Goldenrod	*Solidago sp.*	Cream-edged Dichomeris False Crocus Geometer Green Leuconycta Solidago Root Moth
Grasses		Double-banded Grass-veneer Gold-stripe Grass-veneer Elegant Grass-veneer Snowy Urola Harnessed Tiger Large Mossy Lithacodia
Ironweed	*Vernonia sp.*	Red Groundling
Leaf litter		Orange-patched Smoky Common Idia
Lichen		Lead-colored Lichen Scarlet-winged Lichen Painted Lichen Little White Lichen American Idia
Milkweed	*Asclepias sp.*	Delicate Cycnia
Mint Family		Bicolored Pyrausta Mint-loving Pyrausta

Mustard Family		Diamondback Moth
Plantain	*Plantago sp.*	Harnessed Tiger
Ragweed	*Ambrosia sp.*	Green Cloverworm
Strawberry	*Fragaria virginiana*	Garden Tortrix
Sunflower Family		Zebra Conchylodes
Violets	*Viola sp.*	Beggar Moth
Wingstem	*Verbesina sp.*	Ambiguous Moth

Index

Notes

Notes

Notes

Notes

Notes

Notes

Notes

www.ingramcontent.com/pod-product-compliance
Lightning Source LLC
Chambersburg PA
CBHW041214030426
42336CB00023B/3347